46

Sheila E. Harvey.
See Page 75

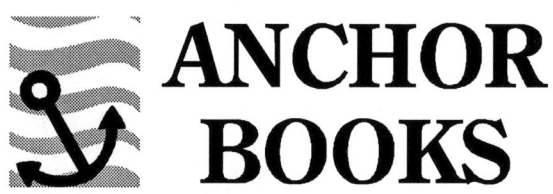

ANCHOR BOOKS

CELEBRATIONS IN VERSE FROM THE MIDLANDS

Edited by

Sarah Andrew

First published in Great Britain in 2001 by
ANCHOR BOOKS
Remus House,
Coltsfoot Drive,
Peterborough, PE2 9JX
Telephone (01733) 898102

HB ISBN 1 85930 941 0
SB ISBN 1 85930 946 1

*F*OREWORD

For many of us the medium of poetry offers us a voice - a voice to speak out and let others know what we feel, think and desire. It is the vital bridge of communication that lets us share our innermost thoughts and messages on life to people who may need that vital surge of poetic inspiration.

Each of the chosen poems have been specifically favoured from a large selection of entries sent. As always editing proved to be a difficult task and as the editor, the final selection was mine.

Celebrations In Verse From The Midlands is a unique collection of poetry and verse written in a variety of styles and themes, brought to us from many of today's modern and traditional writers, who reside in this area. The poems are easy to relate to and encouraging to read, offering engaging entertainment to their reader.

This delightful collection is sure to win your heart, making it a companion for life and perhaps even earning that favourite little spot upon your bookshelf.

Sarah Andrew
Editor

CONTENTS

WEBS

Beautiful death traps wreathed in moisture
from an early autumn dew.
Lovely patterns strung impossibly
catching and reflecting light of every hue.

Too wet for the spider yet to use them,
near to breaking by the weight of water.
Yet dried up shells of the once living hang
as mute testimony to the slaughter.

What a miracle of life and death so closely
interwoven and juxtaposed.
There is no quarter can be asked or given,
just life as it is in the raw - exposed.

Neil Hardy

MOTHER EARTH

Oh Mother Earth, your tranquil land,
with windswept plains and treacherous seas.
Do we look after your coral reefs,
and mighty mahogany trees, evergreen forests too!
Polluted cities and smog filled skies
stretch resources to the limit.
Greed and wealth have become the new breed,
what more of a model do children need.
No longer can we stand and stare, for if we do,
it shows we don't care.
When consciences prick.
Oh Mother Earth, we look forward to baby's birth.
The precious land, for which we all must be preserved
for our children deserve to be able to conserve.

K M Whetton

NATURE'S YEAR

In January, beautiful bare branches
In February, snowdrops appear
March and April bring more bulbs and blossoms
And ere long we'll know springtime is here
In summer the flowers are attracting
Bees and butterflies by petals bright
Come September the harvest is golden
And red poppies show up in the light
By October autumn leaves of bright colour
Are reflected in puddles below
But by November they've fallen, to show up
Red berries which will give birds a glow
It's December, and yellow winter Jasmine
And holly, tell us Christmas is here
We can see frosted grey leaves from the window
And know that soon there will be a new year.

Muriel I Tate

A NICE CUP OF TEA

Whenever I'm feeling depressed and low
And the day has lost its glow.
I put on the kettle, warm up the pot
Soon I'm enjoying my tea nice and hot.

When shopping and working become a bore
When each daily task is just a chore
That faithful old teapot on the table goes
My love for my cuppa daily grows.

It's the best drink in the early morn,
When my wits are fuddled and torn,
It's the best drink at night when work is done,
Gives a sense of well being, all worry to shun.

Champagne and wine are all very well,
At banquets and parties they are swell
On returning home the first thing to do
Is put on the kettle and brew.

When I am called to the mansions above
And St Peter says 'Enter my love,'
I hope he remembers to have a teapot at hand
So we can share a cup with the heavenly band.

Lois Burton

FEBRUARY SNOW

Softly falling from cotton wool clouds,
Drifting silently to the ground,
A celestial blanket embraces the earth
Wrapping its ice-cold arms around
The trees, dressing them in intricate lace
Like brides at the altar on their wedding day,
Numbing them to their very core,
Chilling their hearts in shiv'ry dismay.
Then, as palest sunbeams tickle the earth
Mother Nature commences her miracle birth.
From beneath their shroud frosted snowdrops peep
Waking the world from its wintr'y sleep.
Soon golden crocus will smile on the lawn
A welcome to each spring-breezy, March morn.

Terri Annable

WILLING VOLUNTEERS

Along with the group of ladies I'm doing a course in the belief
That for elderly people we can bring some relief,
By doing some massaging to help them relax their shoulders
We are also massaging their hands, arms and necks to orders,
The name of the course is Therapeutic Care
We have lectures and do practical things while we are there,
About eleven o'clock we have a coffee/tea break and unwind
The instructors towards us are patient and kind,
At Walton Hospital we will be working in difficult places
Trying to turn people into having happy smiling faces,
By our efforts on their limbs and a bit of a chat
About various places on this and that,
We are all willing volunteers so we don't get paid
We're happy if it turns out a friend we've made,
The hours may be small but we hope they'll be fulfilling
As we do our task with people who are very willing,
To be worked on by our magic and tender fingers
And we hope their memory of our kindness lingers,
As they go on their way to who knows where
But we all hope that they remember our tender care.

George Reed

JOKER MASK

I'm a bit of a joker, that has to be said
But I'm crying deep down inside
It's no joke what's deep in my head
Or all the nights I've sat and cried

I can make people laugh with one silly face
Have them in stitches with what I do
I live life at such a fast pace
So you don't see what I'm going through

You think I'm so confident in my ways
That I know not one single fear
But you're not here on my darkest days
That have lasted for many a year

I'm scared but you only see a mask
So self doubting but appear so sure
Afraid of failing the slightest task
Being happy is just such a chore

I'll go on smiling like I always do
Still make the jokes you all love
But deep inside I wish I were you
That's my prayer to God above

To spend just one single day
Treading the path you take
Because no matter what I do
This joker is one big fake.

Melanie Lillian Brown

ANGEL NO MORE

Solid silver,
Shining bright,
I was once full of life.

An angel was what he saw,
But I cannot wear that veil anymore,
It wasn't me, diamonds didn't suit.

You see, I am silver,
I love the moon, and its shine,
And its dust.

That's where I belong, star stepping.

I watch the day break and see it end,
I swim in the sunsets, close my eyes and dream again.

Sylvie Wright

HE IS AND ALWAYS WILL BE

The Lord is our Saviour
Was put on the cross
Millions of people felt his loss

But don't be afraid he said to his flock
Do not judge, do not mock
For I shall arise and be with you forever
My forgiveness will leave you never
The souls who reach out to me
I shall reward with eternity
So stay true and straight my children, fear never
For I shall be with you forever.

Wendy Deaves

CLOSE THE DOOR

Slowly you walk towards the door
Turn the key that releases the latch
You have entered my house, there's an eerie hush
Stopping you dead, your breath you can't catch

The silence shall follow you in this house
It gets louder in every room
There won't be a good time to clear my things
It seems so intrusive, it all seems so soon

Bag all of my clothes, box all of my books
Save the pictures with moments in time
Remove the old clock that hangs on the wall
Within this house it has struck the last chime

Slowly the house is no longer a home
You may weep at the things you may find
Only carpets and wallpaper, the house is now empty
Though furnished with memories, within your mind

A lifetime removed, my effects are all gone
One last look, you shall come here no more
The voices and memories are locked within
As finally you turn and close the door

D Whitehouse

MAGICAL NATURE IN SPRING

Now that the long awaited spring is here
With the sky above so blue and clear
And the wild birds song is what you hear
All around the garden at this time of year

And the flowers awaken from their long sleep
And very soon appear from the soil deep
To create a magnificent colourful show
Around our lawns and gardens as they grow

And soon the leaves appear upon the branches of the trees
And all around the garden are birds, butterflies and bees
And it looks like Mother Nature has just waved her magic wand
And now aquatic life begins to stir within the garden pond

And now we know that the spring is truly here
With all the beautiful flowers that we love dear
And the glorious scents and colours the pretty flowers bring
Together with the melodies and songs the wild birds sing

A V Carlin

SHROVE TUESDAY HANDICAP

They took their eggs and took their flour,
And mixed them with some milk,
They beat the batter with such vim,
It looked as smooth as silk.

With frying pans at the ready,
They stood at the starting line,
Pancakes sizzling in the pan,
They weren't about to dine.

The wintry sun was shining down,
As off they shot without a care,
With aprons flapping at the knees,
They tossed their pancakes in the air.

Old Bessy she just plodded on,
Of winning she'd no hope,
She expertly caught her pancake,
As she slithered down a slope.

Mrs King pushed Mrs Pike,
Making her see red,
When Mrs Plunkett tossed her cake,
It landed on the vicar's head.

During the ensuing fracas,
Old Bessy passed them by a pace,
Just like the plodding tortoise,
Slow and careful won the race!

Pauline Wilkins

THE EYES OF FAITH

Faith is like a candle flame
In this dark world's night
Visibly it grows and grows
Till everything is light
It stills the raging storms of fear
Illuminates the soul
And calms the fevers of the mind
To make the spirit whole
Peace and hope go hand in hand
Companions on life's way
Joined by love and hearts content
When faith is here to stay
Looking at life through the eyes of faith
Is only just the start
To find the strength to cope, and live
With peace and joy in the heart.

Enid Rathbone

A LITTLE ROMANCE

As fragrant blooms that blossom and then die,
So love's first flow'ring dulls and starts to fade;
Awak'ning buds first passions signify,
And young fresh blooms affections thus displayed.
Then diff'rences and apathy belie
Too well the vows and promises once made.

With time affinities are redefined,
Tho' lovers hold their love in high esteem,
And to such changes they become resigned;
But when indifference and coolness seem
To be a second nature, then they find
Those days of romance are but as a dream.

When dreams have paled to which you once aspired,
And life seems cheerless, dreary and mundane;
When all those youthful passions have expired,
And love affords less pleasure and more pain,
Remember well the love you once desired
And bring a little romance back again.

Tho' souls combine it's naive to suppose
That love will thrive, unaided or by chance,
For love needs nurture to ensure it grows:
A tender word, a smile, a knowing glance,
A walk at dusk, a kiss, a single rose;
For tho' there's love, there needs to be romance.

Hilary J Cairns

WHAT DO YOU SEE?

Is the view from your kitchen window pleasing to the eye
Do you look on beautiful flowers, trees that reach the sky
Or are you unfortunate and have no view at all
Except perhaps a concrete slab or someone else's wall

Use your imagination, see what your mind sees
Honeysuckle on the wall, busy bumblebees
Imagine the garden in winter picture all the snow
Or think about the springtime when the flowers grow

That view is what you make it, change it every day
For your imagination will never go away
But if you have a lovely view, see it as a treasure
For it is sure to give you many hours of pleasure

Mary Shepherd

CHAPTER ENDING

How quiet and still it is, like the sea suddenly calm!
A moment ago, forty pupils itched to break loose,
Each to enjoy for a while his own idea of freedom.

All have gone. The tidy room, strangely bare,
Shows no vestige of activity.
A feverish fortnight of holiday-minded children
And of extra duties is over;
Another term, with its mixture of endeavours,
Annoyances, accomplishments, triumphs, is past.

Reasonably satisfied, I leave for home and enjoy the sunshine,
The flowers and trees of the common streets.
The air is full of holiday!

Dora Hawkins

WHEN I WAS A CHILD

When I was a child
we did toast on the fire.

With a three pronged toasting fork
no time to talk!

We looked forward to the treat
after seeing it brown, so neat.

And then did cover it with bacon fat
so how about that!

And then some salt
it was tasty - no fault

And later, now we find toasting is done
in an 8" x 4" box - electric box

But if you go in another room
you will end up with cinders
as black as coal!

Also toast is done on an electric stove
and a gas cooker stove; but beware
of blackened toast if you leave it alone
while watching the tele; without care!

Pity the electric and gas cooking
could not be regulated; it would be smashing!

Marie Barker

ME

I stand still and I look around
What is that thing I have not found
Life is mad, just rushing by
Am I real or am I a lie?
You can't see me, but I'm here
Not your wife, her daughter or someone's dear
What you see is not what you get
Do you realise, we've never met!

I want to sit upon a cloud
I want to shout my voice out loud
I want to dance on fire
But I can't do that, I'm a liar

So life goes on just the same
And I pretend to play the game
I eat, I sleep, I take in air
But no one knows of my despair
Perhaps one day I will awake
I hope I do for all our sake
I feel my dream is somewhere near
And then in time I will appear.

Clare Baker

A Look Over A Garden Gate

Under our feet the soil lies low,
while up above the stars shine and glow.
Up on the hill tops the horses gaze,
while down in the fields the sheep like to graze.
Down in the valley the mist lies low,
while under the bridge the stream will flow.
In the fields the trees will always grow,
while up in the hills the wind will blow.
In the distance the skylark sings,
while in the village the church bell rings.

Katie Barker (13)

No 75 Woodland

In my semi-detached suburban, I went about my chores,
Quite content, I must confess, until 'she' moved in next door.
A mystery this lady, a musical one, at that, teaches the piano,
doesn't have a cat
Not that I'm complaining, but the walls seem mighty thin,
when those everlasting chords go up and up, and down again.
Now if she tickled those ivories with a little touch of jazz,
I might be sympathetic, even be glad.
Maybe she was famous, sometime in the past, now reduced
to teaching other people's brats,
Not big on conversation over the garden wall, I can only imagine!
Why, she is there at all.
Perhaps 'she' (no name) is on the 'wanted' list, moving from town
to town, escaping the wrath of music lovers, who loathe those
awful sounds.
No doubt, I have misjudged her, maybe she's sad and lonely,
or fallen by the way.
One day, I expect, she will vanish, as suddenly as she came,
and I'll be no nearer; solving this little game,
Nor do I know, where her destination may lay, but hope it is detached,
and very, very far away.

I D Welch

THE GOLFER

'Hey Miss, your dog has run off with my ball!'
It was a very loud shout from a boy so small.
'I'm ace at golf,' he confided, 'are you going to watch me play?'
'Go on then,' I said, 'but be quick as I can't stay here all day.'
He whacks the ball, and up flew the dirt, covering his trousers,
his face and his shirt.
My dog chased the ball, with the boy running after,
The air was filled, with his joyous laughter.
He seemed oblivious to the cold and the wet,
Was this little golfer the boy I just met?
His sister shouted 'Your dinner is ready, mum says you have
to come right now.'
'I'd better go,' he smiled 'or I will be in a row.'
When I've had my dinner, and a big glass of squash,
I think my mother will put my clothes in the wash.
'Anyway,' he said confidently, 'I shall be back
and I'm going to bring my brother.'
I thought to myself you will, if you haven't a highly strung mother!
'Do angels have dirty faces?'
Me thinks they do!

Margaret Cloves

WHAT IS ANGUISH?

Nothing is worse than anguish.
Its thrust is deep as soul leaves soul.
A very personal affliction
As love is wrenched from love.

Then anguish, wretched painful grief
Steals far more than your caring heart.
It seeks your whole subjection
Abhorring faith, leaving God apart.

Repel the sadness of the aged thief.
Seek again the realm you both suppose,
Still entwined together to remain
Beyond these Earthly bounds enclosed.

Brian Harris

TRUE LOVE

Although you are many miles away,
You are never far from me,
I think of you each waking hour
And this will always be,
They say parting makes the heart grow fonder
This could well be true,
But darling please remember
This must apply to you,
For courtship is a two-way thing
We both must place our part,
There must be truth and honour
Whilst we are far apart.

Tom Grocott

The Enlightenment

All night I lay awake
Restless, trying to sleep
But sleep eluded me
A vigil, I must keep

As I lay there waiting
Thoughts flew into my head
Elusive and fleeting
Things I had read and said

Then something strange happened
I can hardly explain
But I knew something had
Never the same again

I was filled with power
More an enlightenment
I could do anything
Wherever my thoughts went

I could solve my problems
I could solve world problems
I was filled with wisdom
I had the answers to them

Wide awake and alive
Tingling with new power
With all senses sharpened
I was aglow for hours

I focused my thoughts on
A particular thing
In seconds it was solved
I could solve anything

When the pale light of dawn
Shone over my body
Ready to face the day
Alas! I was a nobody

Terry Daley

WOMAN OF ONCE AND NOW

Once behind loud voice brisk walk and staring eyes
She was soft and slow,
Now she is bold and brash.
Now in some place too distant for rescue
Hides her heart.

Once behind frozen eyes in shadow caves
Another woman lived,
Now sour burned out.
Once behind flesh cold pock marked hard
The skin was silk.

Once behind dry worn lips housed breaths of love.
Now in cracked cheeks
Lodge razor blades,
Savage payment for seekers of more than
Her oft spun dance.

Once behind marbled eyes there lived some hope.
Now with mindless gaze
Time and need have etched,
She bears an ever dying hope's repeat
Of daily hell.

Once . . .
And now . . .

Sylvia Anne Lees

WHY?

I look at your photo, at your lovely smile
And think this can't be real
You're just out for a while
The dogs and the cat sit watching your chair
They can't understand why you are not there
You were so gentle, so kind and so caring
We were happy together, a special love sharing
I know that God called you
And you had no choice
But oh! How I miss the sound of your voice
I love you so much you would tell me each day
I will love you forever, sweetheart you would say
I don't sleep well now my thoughts all a muddle
I so miss your touch, a kiss and a cuddle
At night your whisper in my ear
Warm and safe when you were near
Now when all the world's asleep
I lie awake and often weep
But you're not here to hug me
To say 'Hush babe, please don't cry'
I truly love you sweetheart
Together we'll get by
People tell me 'life goes on'
How I'll never know
Oh! My lovely gentle man
Why did you have to go?
Is this forever baby
For we would always say
That we would be together
Forever and a day.

Rosemary Walker

WAVES

our human hearts beat with a cosmic rhythm
for in the mind resides just a collection of memories
as, in the soul with a body
it is not what we are but what we are searching for
that defines us

we cannot touch a petal without holding a star
nor watch a butterfly seeing our true selves, and
just as the fruit already exists in its seed
we are the huge eternal

in discovering our Spiritual presence
that which gives colour and beauty to this world and makes us, us
we come face to face with this true self
and we are freed
from the duality of You and I:
we become Us

as a wave in brief individuality breaks upon the beach
then returns and merges with the ocean,
we lose identity
and gain totality,
the night of dreams becomes the day that casts no shadows

for there is no permanence, only change
birth and life and death are mere acts in the play,
in becoming our destiny, when
enlightenment sups with the Source,
we realise our own Reality

before time there was just being, yet
we wait and wait for the bondage of time
but if we still the mind and release our hearts,
time ceases
and in timelessness we are perfect

live now, this moment
and we live in Eternity,
consciousness without beginning nor end

and every life becomes a poem

Patrick Ellis

Unique Earth 2001

The moon is shown to be so uninviting.
Planet Mars is simply not to our liking.

Planet Venus is the brightest light amongst the stars
and is unable to support life, just like Mars.

Countless stars display patterns in a cloudless night.
The moon appearing to change shape while reflecting light.

Planets other than Earth have no life to bestow.
Earth is the only planet allowing all life to grow.

Planet Earth is unique and pulsating with life.
Humans can create their own kind of strife.

Compensating for this strife is love, laughter an song.
Where did all the other planets go wrong?

The glowing sun maintains a steady course.
This life giving fire is Earth's only heat source.

The sun goes down and will rise tomorrow.
When the sun stops shining it will be time for sorrow.

Darwin's Theory of Evolution seems right.
Could evolution happen without God's might?

Brian Bates

LESLIE

They arrived from far and near,
Some stone-faced and some in tear,
His son's grey cottage laid heavy with black,
The rain so incessant it muddied the track.

The hearse moved off so slowly and steady,
The cars behind when full and ready,
The tiny church set upon the hill,
Soon appeared through mist, so quiet, so still.

We followed Leslie through arched church door,
Our feet echoed so loud on the cold stone floor,
The service, though good, seemed very long and slow,
If Leslie could have spoken he would have wanted to go.

His friends said farewell with tears and prayers,
Suddenly it was over and we left in pairs,
Outside the rain and the fog had crept in near,
Even the church looked as if in tear.

Wife, sons and daughter, watched as Leslie disappeared from view,
The rest silently waited as if in queue,
When prayers were said and earth symbolically thrown,
We drifted together slowly home,

Not before kind and loving words were passed with friends,
Goodbye Leslie, no more of life's twists and bends,
Lie in peace and thank you for being my brother,
I will go and sit with our dear old mother.

Colin Jones

UNTITLED

I live in a world of ending rainbows,
Fairies and pixie dust.
Of spectres and spirits, giants and gods,
And unbreakable trust.

I live in a world of love at first sight,
Destiny and fate.
Where joy overrules, soulmates are found,
With an over-open gate.

I live in a world of make-believe,
Fantasies and dreams.
Where unicorns prance on pink cotton clouds,
And the sun forever beams.

I live in a world where you don't belong,
You already have it all.
You went out of your way to bring me down here,
So you could laugh at me when I fall.

I live in this world 'cause I can't face the truth,
I have to hide away.
The rainbows and fairies and pixie dust,
Are the only reason I stay.

Kate Weatherall

Untitled

I get such pleasure from little things
Especially when the robin sings
To see him for me is sheer delight
It seems to set my soul alight
A newborn babe so helpless there
I want to take into my care
A summer's day, with breathless view
These mean so much to share with you
The cobweb veil, on dewy morn
The thrushes song as if reborn
To see a loved one's face again
These are joys in my heart remain.

Muriel Rayner

LOVE

It walks on water,
It flirts with the wind,
It lingers in graveyards
And forgives those that have sinned.

It doesn't come in bottles,
It's free to us all,
It's present at birth
And written on subway walls.

Don't throw it away,
Don't sling it in the bin,
It's there for us all,
It's a God-given thing.

You can't buy it Sir
She says with a grin
So - dig deep down
It comes from within.

Sandy F Mellor

BEDTIME STORIES

Losing consciousness
Falling into emptiness, darkness
A coven of endless possibilities
A game of chance
Good or evil
Only the sandman knows,
Has the responsibility for my
Terror or contented restfulness.

A state of REM
Unknown to me, recognised by others
Their ignorance breeding curiosity
Of my visions,
My emotional trip, questioning
Am I being suffocated by
Personal mind games?

Insecurities, desires, fears
Are all part of the jigsaw
I have no choice but to play
Put the pieces together,
Mirroring my soul,
We try to understand the complex
Yet we ignore the simple?

Freedom is to choose
Where is the choice?
I am helpless to fatigue
I am a prisoner of my subconscious.
I cannot fight myself
Therefore I am helpless
I have no choice
But to give into my dreams.

Jennifer Matthews

ONE-OFF

I'm an ordinary person
The type no one looks at twice
I've always been a one-off
Others get the larger slice
It doesn't matter what I do
Or what I try to say
Other folks can top it
Or squash it in their way
It can be so confusing
But I just let it ride
Must not upset the know-it-alls
I would hate to hurt their pride
I'm content to watch them
All struggling to get top
As I can give a wry smile
When I hear a clangor drop

Dorothy Groom

GREEN AND PLEASANT LAND:
GREY AND UNPLEASANT WORLD

I sat in a forest, the sun sprinkled through the trees
Lovely and warm, save for a gentle breeze
That stirs me from my dream
Of England pleasant and green.
But wonder I need not
If all turned their eyes
To the splendour we have got.

For how long it's at present unclear
That we can enjoy our land so dear
Those with influence, money and power
Cover this greenery hour by hour.
Day by day, fields turn grey
Earth turned forever sour
Never again to see light of day.

Rob Purcell

LAD'S LAMENT

The little girl who lives next door
Spies on everything I do
There's a knot hole in the wooden fence
That she keeps peeping through
When her friends all come around
She puts on airs and graces
But when my pals come round to play
She just keeps pulling faces
And if I'm coming home from school
And she's walking down the street
She crosses to the other side
So we don't have to meet
She makes noises at my little dog
Just to make him bark
And throws stones at my pussy cat
She thinks it's quite a lark
She tells my mum I'm teasing her
Which gets me in a row
I don't think she could be nice
She doesn't know just how
I really wish that one fine day
Her folks would up and move
And then perhaps she will realise
We're head over heels in love

Dennis Malin

NIGHT SNOW ON ERYRI

(Snowdonia)

Snow of no colour
  not white
seeding the mountain
  cropping invisibly
brimming like liquid
  night gases
tideless under blackness

Dusted ice spinning
  in secret cavities
where no foot treads
  among cwms and chasms
quilted and rimed
  in perilous silence

John Alcock

SMILE

A smile seems such a tiny gift
But when it comes the clouds will lift
And someone feels that life's worthwhile
Because a stranger paused to smile
But when a frown is put on show
We soon feel sad and full of woe
By showing the world a happy face
We will spread good cheer around the place

May Walker

SILVER

From the window all was grey
not the grey of early dawn,
nor yet the grey of a cloudy, damp
November morning.

It was icy cold, but then the
roseate sun began to rise over the horizon.

The grey leaves, the grey branches and
the grass took on a pinkish tinge.

Dawn brought hope of life.
Gradually the frost
turned to rime.

New shades appeared - blue water,
brown, green, gold.

Branches, and buds
began to glisten;

Droplets fell,
Birds began to drink.

Jane England

WHISPERING WIND

Whispering wind,
Softly caressing
My upturned face,
Look and see my tears.
Blow them away.
Let me see again,
Let me see you,
As you toss the leaves,
All powerful.
Give me your strength now,
While you move on,
To create a world
Where you are God.
God take me with you,
Help me forget,
This world of cruel hate.
Give me new life.
Like the leaves I could,
Dance in the wind,
Until you move on
And I am left
Until the next time.

Julie Allen

MY SON

My son 60 years young today
Keeping his vintage cars to stay
Ready to ride another day
Rain or shine come what may
Friends and family fully understand
He is always ready to lend a helping hand
His wife and he, loving Mum and Dad
The best parents their children could have had
I am a worrier, quite a trial
But I always greet him with a smile
I am lucky to have such a caring son
To make my old age a happy one.

Edna Ballard

SILENT VENGEANCE

How sweet the lies which cover fears
And rectify what you perceive
That cast away your blatant tears
To justify why you deceive
Not lost and nor forgiven
Just slotted in a place to be
Hold tight for which is waiting
For justice is what you will see

My patience is a blessing
A knowledge formed into an art
Through past and fated destiny
I've learned to live the reapers part
For time is on my side now
An inner need I will pursue
Endorse a silent vengeance
No one will hear or ever view

One fact in life that's always true
Destroy some goodness you have found
You will only reap back what is due
What goes around, comes around.

Jane L Smith

CHERISHED DREAMS

I've found it best to write in words
Just what I wish to say
I've also found it helpful
In driving cares away
Tonight my heart is weighed down
And writing fails to lighten
For I'm afraid that we must part
And leave my poor heart broken
It's hard to put just how I feel
And yet I feel like writing
To try and say my loves for you
And stop my thoughts tormenting
We dreamed our dreams in sweet repose
Of children of our own
How sweet those memories linger
How sweet the thoughts alone
It seems as though that we must take
Our dreams just as they come
Just passing thoughts within our minds
Of a daughter and a son
Our dreams are only of these two
They're the sweetest dreams of all
Until we cease to dream these dreams
Our hopes will never fall
But then again this cannot be
Your love I cannot win
But I shall cherish all these dreams
Until my eyes grow dim

C Baynham

SHOOTING THE RAPIDS

The raging river comes into view,
The four of us know what we have to do,
Into the raft with nerves so tight,
Lean into the oars with all our might,
Why did we have to take this on,
Our chance to avoid it is long gone,
Look out, there are rocks just over there,
The raft now climbs into the air,
The sides of the gorge soar into the sky,
And overhead great eagles fly,
Seeming to pause in their mid-flight,
As if sympathising with our plight,
There are two more miles we have to go,
How will we make it? I don't know,
Our eyes are filled with flying spray,
I wish those rocks would go away,
I swear if I can get back home,
I never evermore will roam,
And never will I board a raft,
I'll stick to far more safer craft,
That do not need a raging flow,
To get me where I want to go,
Don't ever show me a river again,
I'll take a bus, a car, a train.

John Earp

What I Wouldn't Do For My Mate Bill

Hold his hand in the playground,
Carry his books to the school gate,
Little Billy Baxter the boy with one best mate.
One square of chewing gum - split into two,
The bigger bit for me but a piece for Billy too.

I save his place in the diner line, so Billy pushes in,
It's only a little place cos Billy's only thin.
I got real big muscles and a hair on my chest,
But I still think my mate Bill, well he's the best.
Billy's good at maths, computers and geography too,
I'm only good when Billy's there, he helps me muddle through.

I see what Billy sees and he sees the same as me,
He's good at describing things it's almost like I can see.
It doesn't really matter to me if I stay the way I am,
As long as Billy doesn't mind being part of my future plan.

I've never seen my mate Bill, I bet he looks real cool:
He's so good at everything especially at school.
He is best at describing things he brings them to life,
If I were a girl I'd like to become, well . . . Billy's wife!

Janet Millard

TOO BUSY

I'm much too busy to stop and chat,
I've lots to do, there's no doubting that.
I know you're my mom, I know I should care,
But for heaven sake mom, I know you are there.
If ever I need, I know you will call.
You'll be there behind me if ever I fall,
But for goodness sake mom, don't want to chat
Because you know I'm too busy for that.

Oh dear, there's the doorbell, let's see who is there,
Great, no need to move, it's mom, she'll not care.
I've asked her to visit but I am so very tired,
So I'll not bother; well I'm not retired.
I work hard all week, deserving a rest,
So why should I bother with her, she's a pest.
She'll always be there at the end of the phone,
Why bother to visit whilst she is alone.
I speak to her occasionally when I need to say,
'Please will you? Or can you? before break of day.
I know she'll oblige, she's that kind of girl,
Cause she loves me I know she will give it a whirl.
The thought she is lonely does not come to mind,
You know that I've said that I'm not that kind.
So for goodness sake mom, don't just want to chat,
Cause I've said once before 'I'm too busy for that.'

Oh God, in his heaven could she be so blind,
To see that I'm busy, I've money to find.
I've bills to pay, the dogs to feed,
The housework to do, the garden to weed.
The lads all need money to go on their way,
And please don't forget, that I need to play.
She's really ungrateful, she asks for so much,
Just every now and again a small tender touch.

Why should she demand so the question I ask,
When my life is full with this pressuring task.
So I repeat once again mom, don't ring for a chat,
Because again I will say 'I'm too busy for that.'

So get on with life mother don't expect me to phone,
You know all this sadness, I'll never condone.
I don't see a problem because I don't call,
Our photos are there, they hang on the wall.
I know they don't move, I know they are still.
So chat all you must and chat all you will,
They're there to remind you of what you once had,
A loving and caring, mischievous lad.
I hope with my heart that I'll n ever regret,
The words that I said that she won't forget.
Don't bother to phone to just want to chat,
Because even for you mom, 'I'm too busy for that.'
These words I have said each time I depart,
To a mom that loves me with all of her heart.

Glenda Burton

Civil War

Wounded, the boy surveyed the battlefield, the flag he held was torn,
Union bodies all around on what was once a lawn,
Through misty eyes he thought he saw the legions gone before -
The men who had fought and died to create American lore (law).

Indian bodies wet with sweat, feathers dipped in blood,
Covered wagons fording steams, running high at flood,
Bearded barefoot men trudging forward to new lands,
Bonneted women planting seed with their hardened hands.

To his ears there came the strains of distant spiritual songs.
The faces rose before him of men who'd righted wrongs.
All these glories haunted the young boy's early dawn
Upon that bloody battlefield which was once a lawn.

Brother killing brother, bonny lads in blue and grey -
Young men who had not so long put their toys away.
In screaming hell, sulphur rides to hasten on an end,
Crying to their forebears each faith and hope to lend.

Daylight fades, the youth is dead in the sweet night air,
With silent ghost-filled eyes the boy is lying there.
Tenderly another friend takes up the tattered rag,
At Valley Forge and Gettisburg he proudly held the flag.

Christine Grainger Brown

STOLEN FRUIT

She, running up,
He, running down,
Collide on the stair,
He touches her hair . . .
His wife wasn't there . . .
A smile in a dream, 'the au pair'.

He, running up,
She, running down,
Again, on the stair,
His wife wasn't there,
Couldn't resist stealing a kiss,
Peaches and cream, succulent bliss . . .

Roger Mosedale

FAERIES

I walked down to the end of my garden
To the furthest possible sight
I was told that I might find faeries
And see them dance on the moonlight
The night was warm and mellow
The moon was shining bright
The stars were in their heavens
A truly magical night
I curled up under the Sycamore tree
And drifted into time
I could hear the tinkle of bells afar
I hoped this was a sign
I waited almost afraid to breath
And afraid to close my eyes
Then I saw a mystical fairy ring
Dancing with fire flies
As I stared with a look of wonder
They beckoned to where I lay
I was being invited to dance with them
To music far away
They took me up to the moon and stars
And showed me a special place
Then they brought me back to my garden
And they were gone without a trace -
I thought I must have been dreaming
Until something caught my eyes
It was my own little pair of fairy wings
Lying by my side.

Jacquie Wykes

Nova - 08/02/01

The lights come up and all you can see is a silhouette,
and hear the revs pacing in time with the bass.
You harness in and start cruising
until you find an open road,
see the blinding flash in the mirror,
palm the wheel, shift down and pop the clutch
to watch the competition shrink on the horizon.
You don't win much! Except for the prestigious
wave of victory as you pass a girl
and let your hazards flash.

Andrew Dowen

CATHEDRAL

Works of wonder,
Workmanship away from the norm,
A voice that speaks,
in the mediated pattern,
of textured stone.
Shape and substance,
Gothic cathedral,
with spirituality.
There is a message in stone,
as much as a scripture
etched on rock.
A core worked monument
of mental receptivity,
with soul inside.
For the sake of contemplation
to strike at a need to express
a whole being,
through aesthetic painstaking personality,
of an age gone by.
A hint, or a reminder of reality
through one passing time
of worked distinction.

Paul Darby

TIME AND TIDE

Time and tide for no man will wait
To ignore that a big mistake
Our ship will sail when tide is high
Or we will be left high and dry
Often with much to lose at stake

Time is something we cannot make
But time is there for us to take
Lost forever if let go by
Time and tide for no man will wait

Sometimes we learn and far too late
Delay leaves us in hands of fate
Lost time for us often deny
That second chance for which we sigh
The choices now are second rate
Time and tide for no man will wait

K W Benoy

WONDERFUL NATURE

A beautiful flower in bloom attracts a busy bumblebee,
this is just one thing, to which nature holds the key.

Building their nests, birds use bits, twigs and sticks,
spiders spinning their webs on wooden posts or in-between bricks.

When the rain as fell, it leaves behind a scent of freshness,
making flowers at their best, sweet smelling more than less.

The sun trying to pass the clouds, it takes a peeping chance,
to bright for the human eye to take a long distant glance.

New shoots appear through the rich soil with ease,
trees swaying pretty to and fro in the gentle breeze.

Nature after all is a wonderful thing, something we take for granted,
without it we would all be lost, because it is greatly wanted.

Donna Marie Stokes

MY PET

He never cares the way I look
Or even how I dress,
And when I'm in his company,
I don't have to impress

He goes around so quietly
When I don't feel too well
And as I look into his eyes
I'm sure that he can tell

When I am eating something
With a smell that he thinks good
I know he hopes I'll leave him some
He'd ask me, if he could

He can never say when he feels ill
Or rub a place that hurts
So mind you treat him properly
And realise his worth

A truer friend you'll never find
He's there no matter what
So just you love him in return
He's not asking a lot

Pearl Ward

THE SLOW SCARECROW

Away black crow
Elusive foe
You sow not nor do reap
Yet swift you swipe
The corn so ripe
When I am fast asleep

Be gone black crow
False so and so
You swindle and you cheat
When it satisfies
To close my eyes
You steal my master's wheat

Take heed black crow
For well you know
Your folly is my fun
Oh! And forgive me dear
For you would not hear that shot . . .
From my master's gun

M I Birch

LIFE IN WEST BROMWICH

Living in West Bromwich
Stone Cross to be precise
People say horrible things about this area
But really it's very nice.

Folk around here are friendly
Will help you if you're in need
Often saying 'Good morning' to strangers
Sometimes we even pay heed.

Buses come every few minutes
You never have to wait for long
Then there's the four pound Family Day Saver
Where four people travel for a song.

Shops are plentiful, no complaints on that score
Tesco, Spar, Safeway, Kwiksave, to name a few
Not forgetting hairdressers, chemists and shoe repair
The ones you go into is up to you.

Happiness will greet you as you enter your favourite pub
Proprietor and regulars welcome you with a smile
You'll quench your thirst and satisfy your appetite
Share conversation with friends, you haven't seen for a while.

Accommodation is plentiful, you can choose
Housing, private or council homes fill the need.
Gas, electricity and water can be connected without fuss
People are on both sides if you want to feed!

Once your neighbours discover you're friendly
You'll be called 'Love' and 'Darling' but take no offence
It's the local form of endearment
You'll find it called from over the fence.

Wendy Marchant-Crawford

FINAL CONQUEST

You are my final conquest
The burning flame of life
You are my pillar, full of strength
Through trouble and through strife

You are a martyr in my life
A milestone I have reached
You harken as I call to you
My words, strong yet beseeched

You are the chapters in my book
That looks and feels so strange
You are the one that walks
Within those winds of change

You are my sheet of music
Your sweetness fills the air
You are the one that I adore
So loving, kind and fair

Helen Sutton-Bradley

HOPE

When you walked into my life, time stood still,
A feeling of elation, contentment, life fulfilled.
Where once was a chasm, so deep and so wide,
A newly found passion now fills the void.

Only yesterday I felt so low and in despair,
But I turned a corner and you were standing there.
Fate has brought us together and now I know,
You'll be there by my side wherever I should go.

Maggy Copeland

COUNTRYSIDE

I kneel down in the grass of green, amid the flowers of blue.
The laughter of my children, echoes through the misty dew.

The sun is trying very hard, to break through from the clouds.
Everywhere around me I hear dawn chorus sounds.

The birds they are all chirping, the cattle give a moo.
The chicks are clucking everywhere, laying egg or two.

The farmer in his tractor, before sowing all his seeds.
Pigs roam around their mucky styes impatient for their feed.

I really love the countryside, I sigh contented sighs.
Then I see the smoky towers, as I open my eyes.

I hear the cars all screeching, I see the smoky haze.
I realise I've been dreaming of country holidays.

K Winsper

MARCH TRAGEDIES - 2001

What a shock, March was here . . .
'Foot and Mouth' bringing widespread fear.
Cattle slaughtered, field fires blazing red,
Flames rising high, and so many dead!
Farmers waiting for *news* they dread
Of their loving animals they reared and fed.
Why, oh why must they suffer so?
Livelihoods gone and families full of woe.

A freak tragedy at Selby with Express and Freight trains
Wreckage piled high . . . a cold stillness remains,
Passengers seriously wounded, several passed away.
A horrendous tragedy, for their souls we pray.
Shocked friends and relatives lost for words to say,
Patiently had waited for their return home that day.
Searching the 'injured list' and then travelling around
In several local hospitals their loved ones were found.

Daily tragedies everywhere, people in despair,
Countries abroad call for help and urgent care,
Earthquakes erupting, buildings tumbling, homes gone
Surrounded by devastation, the survived struggle on.
Rising floods everywhere bring famine and fear
Death and destruction far worse this tragic year.
Bombs, shooting, killing, murders reported on the *news,*
Risking everything, Asylum seekers, *England* they choose!

Silently one morning snowflakes began to fall,
Soft white and fluffy, floating down transforming all.
Scorched earth in fields from flames of red -
This pure white blanket covered the memory of the dead.
Humans cause suffering, through neglect and lack of care
God sends his love and peace to all, everywhere.

Stella Bush-Payne

SANDSTONE CAVES

At seven, I spent all summer awake:
Each night of looking into the compressed mirror,
I saw my own Austrolopithicus.
It wasn't a Triassic Death
But was just as terrifying.

At eight, the sandstone went blunt:
We awoke, concussed, at the foot of the precipice.
I saw my own silica imprint.
They ran a needle up my feet
To ensure I wasn't paralysed for life.

At nine, I had a whistling in my ear:
Each night of listening for a foreboding face
I saw an accusing Cro-Magnon stare,
Standing on the crushing weight,
Peering from the mass of a thousand deserts.

At ten, coming straight at me in a star field,
Each night of mad-staring at ochre curtains,
I saw my hair burnt, sandy sockets:
Swirling with sandstorms and flies,
Eroding by the acidic wind of the hourglass.

Andrew Strange

THE FAERIE WEDDING

What would have been the stroke of midnight
At the time the moonbeams spilled
Like dreams from out of child's slumbers
Into storybooks already filled;
Within the wood, the darkness crawled
On hands and knees, silent and unseen
To take a peek at what unfolded
In this clandestine, enchanted scene.
Throughout the undergrowth they traipsed,
Dressed in red and emerald thread;
Gold and scarlet capes and cloaks
Faerie folks preparing to be wed.
Weaving in and out the trees,
Oaks and sycamores bow low
And spread their silver boughs across
The pathways where the faeries go.
Treading lightly, taking flight
Like sparks and cinders from a blaze,
Everywhere the Little People
Criss-cross in the moon's cool rays;
And make towards the faerie altar
Underneath the steeple and its spire,
Made of gossamer and cobweb,
Drawn towards it by the choir
Of nightingales singing serenades
In the darkling glade, upon their boughs
While the owls and pipastrelles careen wildly
And the faerie folk exchange their vows.

Jonathan Goodwin

AWAKENING TO SPRING

The garden, from its winter sleep,
Throws out its mantle, dark and still.
But I remember how it looked
With flowers blooming everywhere,
And scents which filled the summer air
With memories I shall keep.

No flowers in sight - no sign of spring,
But yet, when looking further still,
Beneath the hedge, and sheltered there,
Are pure white snowdrops, brave and small,
Their slender stems so straight and tall.
They herald spring's awakening.

And perched upon the garden gate,
My favourite robin rests supreme.
He's dreaming now of warmer days,
And flutters down - for food he seeks.
We both survey the scene so bleak,
And pray that spring will not be late!

Joan Mathers

Heart Felt

The darling buds of May
Had been so far away
And now in all their glory
Raise their heads to tell a story
Locked in one small room
It all began when leaves were falling
You can't go on; a new part must be fixed
The doctor gave a warning
But in those hours of waiting
Time sped by, enriched by love untold
Who thought she's be a millionaire
For joy and sweet content had been her lot
The priceless gift that passes understanding
And now the surgeon waits . . .
Tomorrow, will you hold a fairer day
What e'er befalls
Pure gold has passed her way

Edna Wimperis

FEELINGS

We have feelings that come - and feelings that go
Lots of the time they really don't show
We most tend to keep them all locked up inside
Sometimes there are feelings we just cannot hide

There are feelings of love - and feelings of woe
Feelings we have, that just grow and grow
Feelings for loved ones - we can't always express
Then there are feelings which grow less and less

Let's stop and think of all those feelings we get
That we sometimes can't share - and then we regret
Our partners, our loved ones - why can we not tell
Of the feelings we feel, when things are not going well?

Again there are feelings which come over us
We never know why - they are there yet no fuss
A 'song' or a 'memory' can bring them our way
Then they are gone - so strange you could say

With feelings at times, we just have no control
Even though we do know they play a big role
We can 'tremble and shake' a feeling can scare
Yet we know it is natural - a feeling is there

Without our feelings we'd never do half we should
Our lives would be empty - feelings make us feel good
They keep us aware, and so make us recall
That a 'feeling' is given, yes to us one and all.

Veronica Buckby

STORM OF LOVE

I sit and wonder,
In my lonely room,
Why it is, this cloud I'm under,
Crying to the hazy moon.
Why love is like a roll of thunder.

A flash of light,
A cry of the heart,
The image of Love, just a sight.
The distant rumble takes me apart,
The storm arrives. I take flight.

If I could just ride out the squalls,
Brave out the elements,
Drown the mocking calls,
I could be in love from now and hence,
Gather up self-esteem and have the balls.

She approaches through the night,
The clouds disperse,
I see the light,
Knowing my fear's so perverse,
I'm sure to ask, is to be right.

As a rainbow's forming,
An archway of new life,
Our lovers' hearts are warming,
Incredible to believe, a wife,
Could be found for a heart in mourning.

Mike Cranke

CAPE HORN

The crouching lion reaches out to sea
And all who passed have watched each century
Two mighty oceans pound her mercilessly.

What makes us go to such a place and more
To see what Earth's far corners hold in store
A very basic need is to explore.

Most precious gift, to use with thrift, your time
To squander it, is to commit a crime
Your choice of travels can make it sublime.

Your choice of people will be boon or bane
Like fellow travellers trapped aboard a plane
Select them well and rapture is your gain.

Propinquity produces love or hate
A testing journey alters the mind's state
Brings into focus those who'll make your fate.

Look far and wonder at all things you find
This tiny planet will expand your mind
Embrace its peoples and leave fear behind.

Restrict your own horizons and you'll see
The seeds of prejudice will grow in thee
A narrow view of life, your lot will be.

Reject the ways of cows who graze content
A need to risk the unknown is God-sent
Your time on boats and planes is time well spent.

An open mind will guide your path each day
And let your talents, skills and thoughts portray
How you have forged your life, your destiny.

And life a journey starting when you're born
And Death a challenge you can view with scorn
When you have reached your goal your own *Cape Horn.*

James P Kilpatrick

EILEEN'S GOLDEN MEMORIES
OF HER DEAREST DOUG

It doesn't seem so long ago
When we stood side by side
You my dashing bridegroom
Me your blushing bride
How quickly the time has flown
It's now 50 years on
And I still love you darling
Even though you're gone
No longer daily in my life
My love grows more and more
And memories keep you close to me
Love stronger than before
It doesn't take a special day
To hold you in my heart
You are with me always
We are never far apart
But today I think especially
And for you dear Doug I pray
Sending my love as always
On our Golden Wedding Day.

Jean Beardsmore

THE DEMON OF THE WINDS

A wind can be gentle
But be aware,
They can have tornadoes
That can tear

Cows can fly
And houses will fall,
Nothing at all,
Will be standing tall.

Jonathan Ball

BOUDICCA

Her hair like flame is red, but tinged with gold.
Down to her waist it hangs, shining like a flame.
Her skin is pale and fine like the finest porcelain.
Green eyes, bright, piercing, shine with zeal.
Tall she is but yet moves with sensual grace,
Boudicca she is Queen of her Tribe.
The Celtic Iceni fierce, wild.
Tricked by Rome were they to surrender all their lands.
Upon a little mound she stands before the assembled Tribe.
She stands naked which is the Celtic way to prepare
                              for battle or an affray.
Her voice is harsh like the cawing of a crow.
A spear she holds, and brandishes high.
'Come my children' she shouts, 'the time is nigh.
We must kill, burn and pillage
To clear the Romans from our lands
Then, only then, will we see where our country stands.'
Alas, alas, it was not to be.
Kill, burn and pillage they did.
Rome in Britain was brought to its knees.
She and they lost their way.
Their wildness for them would their downfall be.
The might of Rome turned and faced the Iceni Tribe.
Severely they slaughtered, and mercilessly killed men
                              and women in their way.
Proud Boudicca where did she go, not for her a Roman spear.
Neither in chains as a prisoner would she go.
She fled the field in fearful haste.
Into the mists of time she went.
Her time again is yet to come.
The second time will not be the same,
She will return once more and save her race.

Carl Kemper

FEBRUARY FAIR MAIDS

Snowdrop carpets drift into sight,
Spreading blankets of snowy white.
'February Fair Maids', that are found
Even when snow is on the ground,
From winter harshness bring respite.

Pure pearls of whiteness in the night
Guide faltering footsteps to paths aright.
As sharp leaves pierce the frozen ground,
'Snow Piercer' carpets drift into sight.

Beneath the hedge, for our delight,
Snowdrops quiver like doves in flight.
The green-veined petals curl around
'Candlemas bells' that have no sound.
'Heralds of Spring', they shimmer bright
Where snowdrop carpets drift.

Sheila E Harvey

AUTUMN

Morning mists, and golden days
Welcome, Autumn sunshine rays
Leaves turn to orange, rust, gold and brown
As Autumn breezes, bring them tumbling down
Oak, ash, sycamore, beech and rowan trees
Begin to lose summer's green leaves
Acorns, sycamore wings, conker pods, float to the ground
Squirrels scamper, as nuts are found
Leaves lay a carpet, beneath our feet
Children gather them for a treat
We press these beautiful golden leaves
To make a collage, a lovely picture to behold
When winter days are dark and cold
And branches bare stand out, against the winter sky
The 'Autumn Harvest' is gathered in
Sheep will wear their winter coat
And find shelter from the east wind's bite
Birds line up, on rooftops, to fly away
As Autumn colours fade away, Autumn's glorious golden days
All too soon will be, just a picture in our memory
The last summer rose, clings to the briar, reluctant to expire
Berries bright, our hedgerows fill
To feed the birds in winter's chill
A glorious season comes to a close, as skies grow darker
The sun fades away, and leaves our thoughts far behind
When winter winds, blow and wind
That golden picture, fills our minds
When trees turn gold, rust and brown
And sunshine's rays warm our days
In England's Autumn scene.

Irene G Corbett

UNFORGETTABLE

It's that time of year I can't forget,
The time you went away
That awful day the angels came
And I begged them, let him stay.
Nobody heard my cries for help
Or you would still be here
They only saw my sorrow
And my broken heart I fear.
Sometimes when I'm feeling sad
I look up to the sky,
I call your name and talk to you
Always asking why?
I wish that I could hold you
For just a little while
Sometimes I feel you near me
And I give a little smile.
One day we'll be together
So save a place for me,
My heart is yours forever
And my love I give you free.

Loraine Richmond

JAMPOT VILLA

Bright, white, huge and tall,
Please knock, come and call,
Jampot Villa.

All he ever took was jam and bread,
For his 'Snap',
Me Grandad said,
Jampot Villa.

Great thick wedges on his lap,
Me Grandad said,
Jampot Villa.

Great wackin' doorsteps of thick crusty bread,
Me Grandad said
Jampot Villa.

He'd sit there in his dirt and muck,
In the cab of his mucky old truck,
With his jam and his bread,
Me Grandad said,
Jampot Villa.

He'd come out of the gate although never late,
Every morn at the crack of dawn,
With his haversack on his back,
Loaded up with a stack,
Of jam and bread,
Me Grandad said,
Jampot Villa.

Bread and jam every day,
But all me Grandad could ever say was . . .
Jampot Villa.

'He had a lot to say,
Me Grandad did.'

Sally Hunter

THE PIONEER IN ALBERTA

We went to see my father's land
Where he lived long ago.
He died when I was just a babe,
So was not mine to know.

When young he travelled to this place
So wild, remote, no sound.
We found his log cabin remains
And wheat grown wild around.

So many went as pioneers
Before the First World War,
Encouraged by great promises
Of wealth in lands afar.

But he came back to wed his love
And left it all behind.
He settled back to English life
And put it out of mind.

Now I have seen where once he dwelt
Preserved through all these years.
Oh! What a moment of wonder that was
And I was moved to tears.

To think how anyone could face
Such utter solitude,
And build a home and farm the land,
It took such fortitude.

K E Gilbert

UNTITLED

I volunteered early 1943
Joined the WRNS to see the sea
That I did, many oceans too,
And countries, yes, quite a few.

The Royal Naval College, first I went,
To the signals branch I was sent,
Not for long did I serve there,
Drafted, secretly - destinations I knew not where.

During duties in Senior Service bases,
Saw many strange and wondrous places,
Glimpsed deserts, pyramids, camels, the lot,
And King Farouk, never to be forgot,
By the way *'Mahroussa'* was the name of his yacht!

I've seen Scotland, England, and Malta too,
West Africa, South Africa, Aden - and thro -
To Egypt, Palestine, as it was then
Damascus, Baghdad, oh, wasn't I a lucky WREN?

I lived in Port Said with Suez Canal view,
Cairo and Alexandria too
I've seen Aden, the Red Sea, hot there, *phew!*
Visited Aleppo, that's near Turkey, I've never
                    been to *'Albuquerque'!*

Returned home to Blighty late in 1945,
Left the Middle East, with naval pride,
I worked hard, played even harder, toil and sweat,
It's part of my life, I will never forget.

Years have passed, memories linger still,
Until I die, I know they will.
So many wonderful friendships
And hundreds of gorgeous *men*
Oh yes, I was a very, very lucky *Wren.*

Beryl Holroyd-Fidler

UNTITLED

Dear Mother, you are like red rose petals to me
Dearest Mother you are a sunbeam on a lovely summer's day to me
Mother you are like the brightest rainbow to me
With this poem is the only way I can explain my love to you Mother
I love you.

D D-J

JUNCTION 6

Bowed ribbon of noise threading through our heart.
Inhales commuters, ferries goods away.
Carousel meant to speed and not delay.
Oh where and how did the designers start
To unwind this plan, this intricate part
Of Birmingham? Of which one future day
Cause our descendants to wonder and say,
In days gone by Brummies were really smart.
But they will not know these unborn sages
The tension, and what it was like for me.
To sit there in hazed static queues for ages
And ponder in tears. What it was to be
A worker, moving in two-yard stages.
As crows picked rubbish then flew away free.

Tony Brindle

SCAREDY-CAT

Jack Snowden is a scaredy-cat,
He's afraid of everything, and that is that!
He lives in a very rough neighbourhood,
He wouldn't go out even if he could!

Jack is afraid of the bedroom light,
In fact he's afraid of them all!
Jack is afraid of his play toys,
He's even afraid of his ball!

Jack is afraid of the kitchen sink,
(And the bathroom one as well)!
But his scaredyness really makes you think,
Of the scary things that dwell!

Jack Snowden is a scaredy-cat,
He's afraid of everything, and that is that!

Tanya Jade Johnson (10)

OCEAN-LIT DREAM

I feel love all around me
When I'm with this girl
The butterflies in my stomach
The candlelight whirl

The colour of this emotion
Is really hard to find
Personally I'd choose red
But what if you were blind

When I'm eating breakfast
I taste this love so much
The sweet tender flavour
Of her succulent touch

When I think of love
I think of only you
I look upon the starry night
And heaven shining through

I look into my soul
Deep into my heart
The love that is surrounding
Prevents us being apart

When I think of love
And the sounds that it makes
I hear your tender voice
I feel your soft embrace.

G Clarke

UNTITLED

Why is tomorrow never today?
Why does Today always get in the way?
I want to see Mummy,
'Tomorrow,' they'll say.
Oh why does Today always get in the way?

Elias Allen

BACK TO THE FUTURE

The machines of the future,
    destroy the memories of the past.
They are built of plastic,
    and will never last.
Yet we put all our hope,
    into these visions of noise
As we are the children,
    and they are the toys.
But when all's said and done,
    we'll turn back the page
And use the contraptions
    of a bygone age.

Andrew Wright

OUR MOUSE

A mouse we had behind our wall
And late at night we could hear him gnaw.
Then one day he made a mistake,
Out he popped from under the grate.
My shoe came down upon his head
Again and again until he was dead.
My wife cried and sobbed like a fool,
She asked 'How could you be so cruel?'
I then looked down at that mouse so small,
Clean he was, not nasty at all.
How we wish he'd come back to us,
Oh how we would make a fuss
Of that little mouse behind our wall
And we'd make sure that he'd walk tall.

Graham Roberts

AUTUMN WOOD

Gold-leaved beech, dank hanging,
  gold with summer's dying,
Wind-tossed sycamores,
  dresses flying; red.
Earth-crouched scrub, branches chest clutched,
  fallen hornbeams in their grasp.
Yew, proud, defiant still, clothed
  against winter's chill.
Chestnuts, pod burst, clustered
  mid wind fallen leaves,
  hollows haunting.
Carpets, brown, red and gold,
  paths bestrewing,
  spring's grave; dawn of year.
Gentle rain, earth's sobbing for summer lost.
Wind, sighing its De Profundis,
  calls the mourners home.

William Fogg

RAINBOW

Once I saw a rainbow
High up in the sky
I thought it was so beautiful
I wanted to cry.
The colours were so pretty.
I swear this is the truth.
Everyone could see it
As they looked above their roof.
It seemed to last forever
But slowly faded away.
Hidden behind a stormy cloud
To come back another day.

Louise Knight (9)

SPRING

I heard a bird one morn, heralding the dawn.
His lilting song drifting over the early morning dew.
What joy these little creatures bring with their music.
So small and yet so great.

The outstretched branches of the trees, bursting forth
with new green life, greet me as I wind my way through
this leafy glade.

Beauty is all around you, just stop for a moment and
absorb what is happening. God created it all.

Maureen Margaret Huber

To

To be afraid,
But still go on,
When others weep;
Their bravery gone.

To walk alone,
With head held high;
Even though,
Our hearts may cry.

To carry on,
With all those dreams;
'Tho mayhem,
All around us teems.

To do all this,
Courageously:
Means a richer life,
For you and me.

Mary McPhee

BRAVE SNOWDROP

Snowdrop, how delicate, yet strong,
winter winds, will not daunt thee,
through frost and snow, and icy winds,
you dance so merrily,
Snowdrop, you bloom, to spread the news,
that springtime, it is nigh,
and as spring flowers all burst forth,
    Brave *Snowdrop,* then you die.

But sure as seasons, come and go,
and the sea, doth ebb and flow,
Brave Snowdrop, you will bloom again,
    When winter winds do blow.

Jacqueline Claire Davies

UNTITLED

Like the wind, hell rushed in from above.
Aflame with darkness, melting the world away.

Sudden silence - everything stops.
The shadows of happiness fall into the night.

All that was is gone and I am left alone.
Alone in my fear with my memories.

Every time I blink;
The days when the sun once shone.
And I am here upon Arnold's darkling plain,
Where clash by night means nightfall evermore.

Close your eyes.

Block out the light.

You'll find me in the darkness.

Heidi Chinn (15)

FROM GAS TO OAKS

Never such a fool as I
Who walked to town 'neath slate-grey sky
But the paper midst its tales of chill
Said a towpath had been dressed to kill

Black soot soil trod down by toil
Scattered puddles rainbowed by the oil
With duck-like grace I stride to gain
A canal bridge shelter from the rain.

'Gazza Rules' 'The Wolves are tripe'
I wonder what their homes are like
And if they went to school as well
By sixteen perhaps they'd learn to spell

And looking out on a landscape bare
For a missing landmark towered there
The Gas Street Tank, till planners, smart
With explosives tore away its heart

Then young kid with excited eyes
To light his fag, stands by my side
Tells me that he's got a job
At the new car place where the gas tank was

As slits of blue slice slate-grey skies
And cynicism melts from ageing eyes
I see clear path, cut-back hedgerows
As new trees spread young roots to grow

So if Sandwell with black country heart
Beats on to give its young a start
From industrial acorns oaks will be
A young kid showed a fool like me.

Linda Joy Porter

PURPLE AFTERNOON

The grey cold stone of the streets
Bathe in the purple colour of the afternoon
Their wet overcoats glistening
Under the wintry sun.

The graveyard lays out its dormant guests
Their crooked heads now at rest
Await forgotten visitors, bearing gifts
Of thoughts and tears stand and stare
With their prayers.

Surreal in rows too many to count
Display their individuality
Some of grey stone from long ago
Their coats of stone gradually disappear
To the yellow fungi.

Standing alongside the marble choice
Of white and black, shiny and clean
Their gold face-paint glinting in the wintry sun.
The nagging wind, icy in winter
Cooling in summer, acts as a
Guardian to the graveyard guest.

Chivvying visitors around their beds
Licking and stinging faces creep
Into their semi-folded creases.

Careful not to stand on the beds
The visitor is led to dance and jig
Avoiding contact with their neighbours' cribs.

The tombstone maker known to all
His face a feature on each crooked headstone
Will visit no more, as he himself is now a guest.
With monument erect standing tall and
Straight amongst his tidy handiness
Will in time sag and slide to form
Yet another crooked alley.

T J Chaisty